CONSTANT REMINDER
CONSTANT REMINDER
CONSTANT REMINDER
CONSTANT REMINDER
CONSTANT REMINDER
CONSTANT REMINDER
CONSTANT REMINDER
CONSTANT REMINDER
CONSTANT REMINDER

CONSTANT REMINDER
CONSTANT REMINDER
CONSTANT REMINDER
CONSTANT REMINDER
CONSTANT REMINDER
CONSTANT REMINDER

by

GLORIBELL LOPEZ

PEQUEÑAS LIGAS HISPANAS DE NEW HAVEN

Cover Art: *Rompiendo Barreras (Breaking Barriers) II*, work on airbrush, gold leaf and acrylics by Liliana Mejía Sikorski, New Haven Inner City Cultural Development Program (ICCD) artist and a native of Colombia.

Cover design: Liliana Mejia Sikorski, Peter A. Noble

Printed in New Haven, Connecticut, USA by Phoenix Press.

Pequeñas Ligas Hispanas de New Haven, Inc. (PLHNH) is a 501(c)(3) non-stock Connecticut corporation whose mission is to blend the athletic development of children with their artistic, cultural and academic growth.

This publication was made possible with the support from the Connecticut Commission on the Arts, through the Inner City Cultural Development (ICCD) Program, Centro San José, Curbstone Press, Alexander Taylor, Judith Doyle, Naomi Ayala, Liliana Mejía Sikorski and Nilda E. Martínez.

Library of Congress Catalog Card Number: 98-65614
ISBN: 0-9662222-0-2

Published by
Pequeñas Ligas Hispanas de New Haven
257 ~~290~~ Grand Avenue
New Haven, Connecticut 06513   (203) ~~562-3135~~
787-3848

Connecticut
Commission on the Arts

Contents

EDITOR'S NOTE

Those of us in social service are motivated by the small victories that we, in fact, witness daily in our vocation. Some of those small victories steamroll ever so slowly and inconspicuously. Sometimes we get the opportunity to celebrate them pridefully, massively and, yes, poignantly after years of effort.

On June 27, 1996, my friend Roberto Ortiz, former Social Worker and Executive Director at Centro San José, and I attended the Hyde Leadership School's first graduation ceremony at Albertus Magnus College. To us, Gloribell's academic accomplishments were of little surprise. We knew her drive, her creativity, her determination, her social conscience. That night, we proudly celebrated Gloribell's "commencement" into adulthood.

But, Gloribell's maturation had commenced years earlier. Those of us around her witnessed first-hand her unique experiences as a young woman growing up in the Fair Haven neighborhood of New Haven conveyed to us in the form of poetry, prose, drama, essays, paintings, music and volunteer work.

In 1994, I approached Gloribell about publishing her first book. Four years later, **Constant Reminder** is a testament to her courage as an artist and as a human being.

Gloribell speaks from a complex soul. Her words drum like a descarga of congas, timbales, bongos, güiros and cencerros, resonating from the deepest of our being to our fingernails, awakening us from complacency.

Gloribell Lopez is a voice and a role model for those young people who struggle and will continue to struggle with social, economic and identity hardships.

Other rumbas will follow.

Peter A. Noble

Dedicated to my mother

I.

The News in Brief

Good evening. Welcome to the 710th edition of the news in brief. There were only four people shot and killed this week in ****** due to gang and drug related situations. Only 12 unwanted pregnancies, 5 of which have contracted the AIDS virus. Just two racial riots broke out this week, which resulted in only 3 deaths and 14 injuries. 250 people were laid off this week, an enormous improvement from last. Two 13 year-olds were arrested today for the illegal use and sale of cocaine and marijuana at ****** Jr. High School. Only 5 homeless people were found frozen to death in front of a shelter which was closed down due to insufficient funds. Justice was finally served when Anna ****** stabbed and killed her abusive husband. Her two young children, in terrible shock, have been placed under special care. Also a surprise, there were only 25 endangered species wiped out this week, not including thousands of medicinal plants and flowers which were wiped out by construction down in the rain forest of Brazil. Yes, it's been a slow week for the authorities this week and for everyone here at the station. I think things are finally looking up for us. We just might make it. Hope you all have a good night. Please join us tomorrow, same time, same station.

I Know

I can tell you the stories
I can speak of the tales
And boy will you laugh
You might even cry
I can tell you 'bout life
In its strangest forms
Life in its uncertainty, its rarity
Oh and you'll laugh
Shocked by its odd ways
Its sudden miseries
Try and hold back those tears
As I tell you about the time when...
Ah, I remember the hurt
It lasted for a long time
Don't be discouraged
For life's quite an adventure
Quite some surprise
When it strikes you with its daring challenges
Yes, you'll get hurt
But the healing is worth the hurt
Did I ever tell you how I...
Well, anyway I shouldn't be saying
So much
You mustn't lose yourself
I'm warning you
Steer clear of all the confusion
Deceit, unrealistic expectations,
The chaos. The list goes on forever
Be sure of yourself and what you stand for
Remember to...
Nevermind. You'll know what to do
I have faith in you

You'll do fine
Now I know I've said too much
I don't want to ruin it for you
Don't want to spoil all that fun
There's plenty of madness out there
Foolish, unexplainable things
Don't get frustrated
You won't understand most of them
Hell, I didn't
I know I will never understand
I can't say anymore
You have to trust your instincts
I can remember when
Oh, if you only knew

Soul No More

Too blinded by our own existence
To see the beauty that each person possesses
Caught up in monotonous demands
Everlasting expectations

Too deaf to hear the poignant cries
Ability to perceive with our hearts
Has been annihilated by our own
Narrow-minded knowledge

Unable to feel the pain
Feelings pushed aside by rational explanations
Reason, justification
Have prevailed over emotion

Vision has been blurred
Hearing impaired
Feeling destroyed
Soul no more.

Heartbreak

Head hung low
Threats of a tear
Crimson-colored cheeks
And a solemn expression
The heart howls in pain from
A vicious blow inflicted on
The once naive, innocent organ.

Freaks

The sun's down
And the freaks are out
 Out searching
Looking for belonging
Wanting acceptance
Desire to be loved

The night is here
And the freaks are out
 Out laughing
Laughing at the common people's scorn
Enjoying the rebellion
Living for the joyful darkness that surrounds them

The night is clear
And the freaks are out
Sharing their sorrow
With caring silence
Silent understanding
Hand in hand. Too many to count

The day's dead
And the freaks are out
Out recruiting
Signing up is easy
Retiring is prohibited

Racism

No one to blame
The seed has been sown
The hatred is breeding
The ignorance, thriving
The anger consuming
The weakest of minds

Senses

I took a look at death today
Saw it running
Running fast
With flames at its heels

I heard the voice of death today
Screaming amongst the rubble
Which used to be a foundation
A foundation now a grave

I felt the stab of death today
Jabbing at my back with a weapon
And demanding more
I've got no more to give

I'd the chance to smell the stench of death today
Hazy and smoky in my lungs
Thick, enclosing the air
I coughed and choked
My stinging eyes watered

I heard that death disguised itself today
It took the form of passion
And entered into the dimness of the room
With heated desire
It left them both with a slow, deteriorating fate

I saw the face of death today
Reflecting off the streaking
Tear of a small child
A child too young to understand
The world of the living dead

She Smiles

Nervous relatives pacing around
Frantic nurses injecting needles
Pale, white sheets that match her
    smiling face.
The decaying flowers on the side
    of her bed
Heavy, short gasps pleading for air
Her heart beats slowly; as she
    smiles
The thin, limp arm, lost in a tiny
    plastic bracelet.
She stares through us as if
    seeing an angel
Or maybe a saint; and she
    smiles
The frail face pressed lightly
    on the pillow
She will soon be gone, and she
    can feel
Her body losing her soul, and
She smiles.

      Dedicated to the birth and death of a lovely
person I once thought I knew.

Quite Frankly

1. <u>Untitled</u>

If this is a game, then I want to play.
If this is a joke, then I want to laugh.
If this is a lesson, then I want to learn.
If this is my life, then I am happy.

2. <u>Betrayal</u>

She smiled. They smiled back.
She joked. They laughed.
She shopped. They tagged along.
She cried. They turned away and left.

Stared at,
Rejected,
Laughed at,
Scorned,
Judged,
Labeled,
Confined,
Hated,
Feared,
Loved.

You

You with your demands.
Your selfish finger extends toward my shameful
face.
Your merciless accusations hurled at my huddled
     frailty.
You build walls around me.
Encage me.
Suffocate me.
Squeeze my soul for every last breath.

Somehow, somewhere, strength remains.
Patience and timing essential for my existence.

I know my way out.
I know how to be free.
I must wait for the right time.
The right moment.
The precise second when

I leap from my doom into my real being
My real self
No more strings
No more chains

Salesman

Fills the night with promises
Fills the heart with dreams
Hopes for the future
Clear views ahead
Creates confidence
Beams lights of happiness across the face
Erases insecurities with assurances
Doubts with love
Convincing propositions
Attractive notions
Goading glimmers in his eyes
Comforting sincerity
Passion and intensity
Ties the knot of the blindfold
And, when removed,
Fills your mind
With dull, aching realization
And your eyes
With tears.

II.

Glass

"Go. Go. Go. Go!" the crowd cheers as Nick gulps down the last beer. He can still make out the number of empty mugs in front of him, although they seem to duplicate before his eyes. His senses seem to have lost their abilities. Lost control. Feeling somewhat queasy and nauseous, he tries to stand up but doesn't succeed. His quivering joints have also failed him. His weak, wobbly corpse seems incapable of even the simplest tasks. Nick then distantly hears his pals' monotonous chanting begin again as another mug is placed before him. Its force is unbearable. Its power overwhelming. The glimmering shade of gold flashes maliciously across his face. Yearning for Nick's trembling grasp. His cloudy vision plays games with his coordination as he tries to grab the bubbly paradise, and ends up knocking it off the worn, chipped, mahogany bar. The sound of shattering glass is followed by immediate grunts and groans of disappointment. Nick's back is suddenly receiving comforting pats that are followed by "good goings" and "hey, at least you trieds." His self-esteem seems to have shattered among the pieces of glass that now lay on the floor. The glittering pieces now reflect betrayal. The worst is over. Initiation complete. Tomorrow it will be someone different. Tomorrow Nick will be part of the pep rally. He'll cheer instead of drink. What is really important to him now is getting to his apartment without making a fool of himself.

Failure greets him once more. He has somehow managed to misplace his keys and soil his pants. Aside from this, he sees Mrs. Daville (from apartment 6C) turning the corner of the hallway. Nick is sure she has spotted him. There isn't any way she or anyone else could've missed him. A distasteful lump now rises in his throat as he chooses not to give Mrs. D. much thought. He knows he'll be the topic of conversation in one if not many of her Tupperware parties. And sure enough the landlord's wife will hear. Not that it bothers Nick. If they haven't gotten rid of him yet, there's no way that they are going to now. Nick finally manages to stand, (without much ease), when he feels a sharp object pierce his back. When he turns he finds that the prickly object is a bony finger, connected to a pale hand which belongs to the body of an interesting-looking person who stands in front of him. The man is 25, but Nick is fooled by his appearance. He has a small figure but strong features. His limp, shiny, jet-black hair hangs loosely over his deep, dark eyes. The man's jutting cheekbones seem to be propping up his sickly, pale skin. The contrast between his hair and face makes Nick's eyes swim, so he quickly turns away.

"Excuse me. Uh, I just moved here, and I was bringing up some bags in the elevator when I saw these keys lying there. I thought maybe you'd know who they belong to." A familiar clump is held out in front of Nick by the feeble-looking stranger. He instantly seizes the keys.

"They're mine. Thanks. I'm Nick. I don't usually look or smell like this. Just hanging out with a few friends and I got a little carried away. Thanks again for the keys. I'll, uh, see you around or something."

While Nick fumbles with the disordered heap, he feels the stranger's presence still near. The stranger's eyes burn holes through his thin shirt. Nick slowly turns around and witnesses an abundant amount of sorrow and weariness in the man's eyes. Pleading and longing for something or someone. Nick pities the poor man and shines a sympathetic smile, which is followed by a friendly invitation.

"Why don't you come down to the pub with me tonight? I'm meeting a few friends. I'll buy you a beer or two. Whatta you say? Maybe around eight?"

"Sure. That'd be fine."

Nick sees him force a tiny smile and walk away. Thinking his job has been done, Nick turns away but feels the need to look back. This pathetic man seems to have some sort of dominion over him. There's an odd aura about this man. The force that appeals to his curiosity is unbearable. This so-called stranger seems to have stimulated a sensitive part of Nick's memory. Nick remembers his brother Sean. Having thought of it, if this man had some color to his cheeks, he would be an accurate replica of his kid brother. The stranger had the same deep, dark stare that Sean used to have. The shaggy hair was also a part of Sean that was used as a hideaway from the rest of the world. Nostalgia sweeps over him, and he can hardly stand against his unlocked door. Nick doesn't know whether this is the effect of the alcohol or the reminiscence of his dead brother. Sean has been dead for seven years now, and this is the first time since then that Nick finds himself thinking about him. He never knew why Sean had chosen to self-destruct, to commit suicide, but had a few good guesses. He had always been an outcast. Mom didn't pay him much attention. Only when he needed to be bailed out for drugs, among other offenses. Dad hated him. He skipped town when he became aware that Sean wasn't half his doing. Mom messed up when Dad was out of town. Sean was the scapegoat. After that discovery, everyone just sort of despised him. He was at fault for the deterioration of the family. Nick remembers how much Sean was made fun of, the times he had been forsaken, rejected, refused. The lump in his throat is back now, but this time it is followed by the warmest, most conforting tears that have ever trickled down his face. He suddenly realizes that he hasn't even gotten the man's name.

Later that day...(knock)

"Come in," Nick bellows from the bathroom. Feeling a whole lot cleaner and dryer, Nick smiles at the progress he made since this morning. His hair is neatly combed, his shirt neat and pressed, and his pants clean and dry. Even his stomach has settled after a healthy meal. As he walks towards the door, he sees the stranger standing there sporting faded jeans and an oversized sweater. His hair is combed out of his bright eyes. His face is expressionless, though Nick can sense the anxiety of the stranger. The guys at the pub will definitely enjoy this one.
"Ready to head on out?"
"Yeah," the stranger replies.
As they walk down the quiet semi-littered street, Nick allows his curiosity to take hold.
"So, where are you from? What do you do?"
"I'm from Rhode Island. I'm an artist."
Nick then stifles a laugh as he thinks about

the guys' reaction when he brings this man through the door.

"Oils or water?"

"Neither," he replies. "I'm a make-up artist."

"Oh really?" Nick tries to meet with the stranger's glance. He wants him to recognize the humor. Already the taunting has started. And although he hasn't admitted it to himself yet, Nick feels sorry for the man. Almost ashamed.

"Have you done any big-time actors?"

The stranger's unexpected grin disturbs Nick.

"No. I do dead folks. I get a weird kick out of making them look as though they are still alive."

Nick's flabbergasted expression makes the stranger feel confident, amused.

At the pub...

"Hey, guys!" Nick spots the group and hurries to them with the stranger tagging behind.

"How ya holdin' up Nick?"

"What's happening?"

"Hey, what's up?"

The greetings stop and the staring starts. Nick still doesn't know the stranger's name, but none of his pals seem to be interested. They have already placed bets to see how much this guy can hold. They get so caught up in this alcoholic ritual that Nick doesn't think that they consider him part of the group. Nick's skimpy wallet pleads for mercy and states that he'll have to sit this one out. Although he is somewhat disappointed, he's anxious to find out what happens.

"Well let's get started. Take a seat."

The excitement builds as the row of mugs is placed on the bar. The glistening mugs throw wild, captivating reflections into their vivid, eager eyes.

"Go. Go. Go." Slowly and methodically their goading pleas echo into the stranger's ears.

Minutes later...

The stranger has held quite some beer now, and he seems to be losing his stability. His fine, black tresses now look scraggly and filthy. His bright, cat-like eyes can hardly be seen behind the puffy lids. The once pale, porcelain-smooth skin is now blotchy and sagging.

"Go. Go. Go!" they chant.

The shame starts to crawl around in Nick's system and is now a cancer spreading and growing into the worst fear and guilt he has ever experienced. Nick's hands wobble nervously, then tremble uncontrollably. A cold sweat and stinging tears threaten his flushed face. Short, gasping breaths seem to choke him as the guilt sweeps over him in enormous waves. No longer in control, Nick leaps and thrashes his bulging arms towards the frosty mugs. Silence breaks out as the crowd waits for the piercing, shattering sounds of glass to diminish. Numbness now restrains him for an instant. Then slowly, but dramatically Nick makes his exit, ignoring the disappointed grunts and groans.

III.

Scene 1

She takes one last look at what she thought would always be there. The tears cloud her vision, and as the memories fade, she takes an uncertain step into the darkness ahead. Not complete darkness, though. There's a dim lightpost up there. Knowing there's a way out, but not knowing what it is or how to get there, she keeps walking. Hoping that he doesn't notice her shivering. Hoping that she will hear him calling to her. It starts to rain harder now, and her face is cold. Not realizing how far the lightpost is, she keeps walking. Pausing for a split second, she hears a car pull away. Shutting her eyes as if to block out the sound, she raises her head to the night sky. The lightpost, as if on cue, flutters uncontrollably and flicks off.

The Glove

Its bulky figure attracts me from across the bedroom. As I walk towards it, I begin to notice its familiar figure. When I inch closer I see its worn material and faded buckle strap. As I dare to move ahead, I begin to smell its aroma. It smells like thousands of beads of perspiration and moist, supple soil. I reach out to touch the decaying leather and feel the aged creases that dig deep into the fabric like tiny daggers. Shocked by the image that this glove portrays, I retreat my hand and leave the room.

September 14, 1993

The Glove #2

Being attracted to the glove once again, I can sense my perspective beginning to change. The dull, earthy-colored table now props up a smooth, ebony object. The glove now possesses soft and comforting leather. Wild goosebumps run up my arm as I run my fingers across the thin but supporting stitches. As I fit my hand into the glove, I suddenly feel the glove shelter my hand and become a new layer of skin. I smile as I leave the room, feeling the warmth and comfort that this glove willingly gives.

September 15, 1993

The Sentence I

Before I wake up my foggy dream is shattered by
the shrilling sound of the alarm clock in my room lit
by the early morning light forcing its way through
the half-shut blind I nearly was because I just
remembered I forgot to take out my contact with
my friends yesterday was cool outside the wind was
blowing hard to talk to them about the present
when they were part of my past the old hang-out
spot our names were still on the wall now has a ray
of light that is getting bigger so I know it is time to
get up and get moving across the floor was a tiny
spider making a home is where my mom is singing
an old Spanish song I loved him but he never knew
how much stuff I bought that I didn't really need to
see my brother before the end of this weekend was
so strange to be with everyone again after so much
time to waste on an afternoon of sitcoms about fake
families and fake kids who always get their fake
problems fixed in a half-hour till nine so I still have
time before the light fills my room enough for
cousins to spend the night because my uncle doesn't
know when to stop tilting the bottle was too warm
for the baby and now Mom is trying to calm her
down the street Quarter-Man now begs for dollars
so I know things have changed my clothes but none
seem to fit right now it's time to brush my teeth
gleam while I look in the mirror and realize that I
seem different from before.

The Sentence II

One morning I woke up to the shrilling sound of the
alarm in my ear shattering any memory of a foggy
dream-like state I was in my room lit by the early
morning light forcing its way through the half-shut
blind I nearly was because I just remembered I
forgot to take out my contact with my friends
yesterday was cool outside the wind was blowing
hard to talk to them about the present when they
were part of my past the old hang-out spot our
names were still on the wall has a ray of light that
was getting bigger so I knew it was time to get up
and get moving across the floor was a tiny spider
making a home is where my mom is singing an old
Spanish song I loved him but he never knew how
much stuff I bought at the mall that I don't really
need to see my brother this weekend was so strange
to be with everyone again after so much time to
waste on an afternoon of sitcoms about fake families
with fake kids that always get their fake problems
fixed in a half-hour till nine so I still have time before
the light fills my room enough for them to spend the
night because he doesn't know when to stop the tilt
of the bottle was too warm for the baby because
now Mom is trying to calm her down the street
Quarter-Man now begs for dollars and that's when
you know things have changed my clothes but none
seem to fit right now it's time to brush your teeth
gleam while you're looking in the mirror and realize
that you seem different from the other
one...morning

IV.

Choices

You get up at 6:00 am. You're out of the shower by 6:15. You get dressed and ready by 6:30. Then you approach the refrigerator with careful ease. Once again you are faced with the taunting decisions which plague your life every morning. Coffee and toast, or coffee and a bagel. There. Sure, that wasn't that hard. Wait! What are you going to put on the bagel? Butter, cream cheese, nothing at all? Caught up in the turmoil of confusion. Torn between the simple decisions. Choices. We make them every day. Subconscious, meaningless ones that can decide our fate and future. Life-threatening, urgent ones that create stress, pain and suffering and sometimes utter joy and happiness.

What are choices? According to Webster's Ninth New Collegiate Dictionary, choice means the opportunity or privilege of choosing freely. According to society, it's doing whatever you want, whenever you want. Freedom of choice and choosing well is stressed at the Hyde Leadership School. To me, it's about what my life is based on.

Throughout history, countless decisions have been made that affect the way we live today. The Constitution, Bill of Rights, even Civil Wars and Revolutions have made an impact on our lives. If we face our future remembering our past and working with the present, we can avoid or better solve simple, everyday problems.

There are many things that influence us to make the certain choices we make. We are sometimes pressured by our peers to take a sip or just one drag. We are influenced by our parents and teachers to achieve our best. Society has also played a part in our decision-making process. Many times people become discouraged by the negative aspects of their environment, and they put off trying to help it. Sometimes they become part of the problem instead of the solution.

I think that in a lot of ways I am fortunate to have the type of teaching and training I need to be able to have good judgment when choosing. In the sixth grade, Social Development was being taught to me, and one of the lessons was the Problem-Solving chart. There were five steps. These were: Stop, calm down, and think before you act. Say the problem and how you feel. Think of lots of solutions. Think ahead to the consequences. Go ahead and try the best plan. Do these actually work? Well sometimes, for certain people, they can work.

Some of the choices that I have made in the past make up what I now consider my values. I decided to stay away from drugs once I saw the effects they had on people. I want to graduate from high school and college before I get married. All of these decisions have been influenced by my mother, the bravest person I know, and my teachers and friends. I fear the future in some ways because I'm unaware of how I'll react to certain situations. I realize that one mistake could mean my life, or change it drastically. Having learned different steps and processes, and feeling I have a lot of knowledge when it comes to decision-making, I still am the most indecisive person I know. (I even had trouble choosing a topic! Hard to believe!) I still have a lot to experience and learn about this corroded but sometimes pleasant earth, and I'm looking forward to doing that. It is now your time to decide whether or not this paper deserves a good grade. If it were my choice...

Many Factors Involved in Education

My first reaction to writing an essay on education was — "Education?" After giving it some thought, I realized that my reaction toward the topic was one that was popular among many.

There are many sensitive and probing issues dealing with education and its importance. The conflicting views about how to effectively express and encourage the importance of pursuing an education come from many influential sources.

Our parents, friends, teachers, and society can become the forces that sway our personal views about this topic. One opinion that is shared among most people is the one which is the most important: recognizing there is a problem with our system of education, if not many problems. This is the first step to combating the problem.

I believe education plants its roots at home. From learning to say "Mama" and "Dada" to tying shoes, and eventually looking both ways to cross the street, people are always learning. Therefore, parental involvement in their children's education is vital. If children see their parents devoting time to their education, they are more apt to also devote some time.

One enormous and sometimes deciding factor in a person's "education" is the opinions of one's peers. Peer pressure is one of the most powerful influences over a growing child. Gaining acceptance from peers might become more important than doing what's right. Many times students may associate with kids who consider school boring and useless. In turn, they bring other students down with them.

Most kids aren't doing well due to the lack of motivation or interest. Some have admitted to feeling "lost" in class or "stupid." This needn't be looked upon as problems in the school, but as cries for help. Many seem to do poorly because they haven't received the encouragement they need to build confidence. Maybe the student hasn't had the chance to be in an environment where learning is considered positive and fulfilling. These are some of the issues that may be affecting kids' approach or attitude toward education.

With parents committed to their children's education, and with kids sitting in their chairs, ready to learn, we need teachers to teach how to think and learn, rather then regurgitate.

There are many teachers within our system who believe that teaching is just a job to pay the bills with a focus toward the money instead of the students. Teachers then become a negative influential model for the students. If teachers approach a subject with little interest or motivation, it trickles down to the students.

In addition, there are other prevalent issues that touch on education. There have been cries of racism, inequality, and ignorance. Many students in inner-city high schools feel the tension that is produced when they see other kids from suburban schools with more books, resources, equipment, and classroom space. They feel the tension when they see newspapers filled with vicious stereotypes and prejudices hurled at their schools. The negativity becomes yet another wall between students and their education.

I have experienced all of these pressures, yet, have developed enough strength to continue pursuing an education. People must realize that education is a way of gaining knowledge, which is the most powerful tool needed to combat everyday struggles. Education has helped me set and create goals and gain a purpose for life. Without it, I wouldn't be able to further my understanding in life.

Education affects people of all ages, creeds, and races. It affects our future, our country, and our lives. We all play a part in making sure our system of education is working. We must realize that education is more than books and pencils. It possesses a value that cannot stand to have a price tag. It demands time, effort, and dedication to make it perform well. Its demands are getting stronger, fiercer, and too loud to ignore.

This essay first appeared in the June, 1996 issue of <u>The Progeny: Voices of Greater New Haven Youth.</u>

Monsters, Giants, and Superheroes

All our bags had been tightly packed into the back of the small gray car parked in front of an ice-cream shop. We wiped the sweat off our brows, checked that every one was paid and accounted for, and heaved heavy sighs. After a whole month of stressful planning, we were finally ready to go. We were on our way to an intellectual, spiritual, personal, and friendship-building retreat, when suddenly I felt a strong craving for ice-cream. I ran into the store and stood in line behind two kids. They were with a woman who appeared to be their mother. I looked up at the selections and silently made my decision. I patiently waited to order. A couple of minutes passed and the line hadn't moved an inch. The kids couldn't decide. Mesmerized by all the different buckets of different flavors and trays of bright, sweet, and crunchy toppings, they stood open-mouthed and excited. The line grew, and the mother's face turned a dark shade of pink. "Um... uh...I want... a... vanilla...no strawberry... and sprinkle. . . no-" My friends called to me, and the line shuffled, and the mother scowled. I looked at my watch, at my friends outside, at the kids, and smiled.

The life of a child isn't that complicated. They eat, play, color, and sleep. They are in a world of Easter bunnies, Santa Clauses, and Tooth Fairies. They tell time according to what cartoon is on t.v. at the moment. They love Mommy, ice-cream, and birthday parties. They giggle, scream, cry, run, jump, and claim to be superheroes. Doctors, psychologists, teachers, and parents have tried to figure them out, and have come up with stages, explanations, and theories of why kids act the way they do and how to discipline them to act differently. Truth is we're nothing but giants to them. The only things that we probably understand about children are their needs and fears. There are countless parenting books on bed-wetting, nightmares, schooling, feeding, and nurturing. We want to confort and care for them. We are responsible for their welfare. We plan ahead to provide for them. We long to protect them from the monsters.

With frazzled hair we run around doing errands and chores while kids run around with sheets around their necks as capes, and broomsticks in their hands as magic swords. In their universe they are battling against the forces of evil. In their minds, they are capable of anything and everything. They defeat the bad guys that make mommy cry and daddy work so much. They fight inequality by holding hands with the new girl "from a whole 'nother country where it's always hot and people always have a tan." They fight apathy by consistently pulling on your arm and asking "Why?" They battle violence by crying and telling mommy when it hurts. They fight loneliness with a hug and a smile. They increase awareness by "oohing" and "ahhhing" at even the smallest ladybug. They fight superficiality by telling the truth. They conquer stress by tying capes around their necks, grabbing their swords, and shrieking at the top of their lungs until they topple over from laughing so much.

In a world of giants there exist gnomes. They always look up at us. They watch and admire all the grown-up things we do. They scurry about, giggling and singing and being small. They bug us, love us, and need us. They are stuck in a world of giants. It is only when they imitate our senseless ways that we realize how silly we really are. They cling to our pants and hide when confronted with insecurity. They long to be picked up and held, to see what we see. To be tall. It is our job as giants to bring ourselves to their level as well as to pick them up to see ours. Ironically, they long to be big like us while we secretly wish we were like them again.

Monsters. They are everywhere. Under the bed, in the closet, at school, next door, in the big alcohol bottles locked in the cabinet is where they hide. They hide in a push, a punch, an insult and a yell. In the dark and in hunger. They are big and ugly, and kids are faced with them every day. Monsters can keep kids awake at night, but kids can conquer these monsters with the help of a parent, teacher or a friend. Or they can be hurt by them. Monsters aren't fair, funny, or kind. Some linger, destroying the very essence of a child's innocence and spirit. Others continue to surface in people who the children have learned to trust. This is probably the only thing that confuses children. They can't understand why monsters exist and why they can't leave. They can't understand why we let the monsters scare them time and time again. Each day they battle and defeat these monsters without knowing. Their weapons are strong and effective. They use their smiles, their inquisitiveness, their love, their playfulness and energy, and their innocence. With their lives they show us the obvious difference between good and evil, innocence and ugliness, love and hate.

Kids are difficult to figure out. No matter

how much we try to analyze and categorize them, they will always surprise us. We cannot understand how easily they can have us fuming and screaming one minute, and smiling and hugging the next. We don't understand where they get the silly songs and phrases and why they must repeat them at least a hundred times a day. We question how, when they get to bed really late and wake up really early, they still manage to have all that energy. And why it takes so long for them to decide what flavor of ice-cream they want. We wait, maybe not patiently, but lovingly. We wait because in them lies our future. We wait because rushing would ruin their youth. We wait because we know that later they will thank us for waiting. Because childhood is precious and shouldn't be rushed.

I waited in line for about 15 minutes, and after the two kids finally decided what they wanted they received their sweet, cold rewards. Then they looked at each other, at those behind them in line, at their relieved mother, at the disgruntled lady behind the counter, back at their melting treasure, and giggled. The retreat that weekend was great. The anxiety, stress, and preparation right before was a tough battle and a hard fight that was defeated by two toothless ear-to-ear smiles.

Education Was the Deviant

"Deviants never exist except in relation to those who attempt to control them."

Stephen Pfohl
IMAGES OF DEVIANCE AND
SOCIAL CONTROL

As I held my mother's hand on the way to school, I was oblivious to the world around me. I never wondered why we lived where we lived, or why the rest of the students giggled and pointed when they walked by our class, or why mom would always stay up late at night, crying. Spanish was my primary language. I was part of the bilingual education program that met in the basement of my elementary school. It was through the school system that I began to experience (notice) the "difference." Accents were made fun of, so learning English became easy.

As a child, I lived in an inner-city neighborhood surrounded by other families in similar circumstances. I was accustomed to the different customs and traditions that shaped my life. You could always hear merengue blaring through the windows of one of the apartments nearby. Trips to the nearby community center for blocks of government cheese and canned goods were part of our life. I felt very sheltered and loved despite the violence, drugs, and "lack of" that existed in my community. I felt normal. In my neighborhood and in my immediate family I was also considered normal. Although I was happy, my mother would emphasize that there were lots of opportunities for us to be truly happy. She was always stressing the importance of education so that we could have "a better life than she had had." I had always wondered as a child what was so horrible about our life. It was only during the beginning of adolescence that I began to notice the differences in the lifestyles of different people. I wanted to do better than my local over-crowded, bug-and-drug infested high school, and this "want" in itself was a catalyst for opposition. Because of the district that I lived in, I was unable to apply or attend safer and more challenging schools. It was when I began to question that I was considered "rebellious." I began to challenge the institutions around me. I noticed the difference between my family and the ones on TV. I saw their homes and schools, and I was disturbed by the contrasts. It was wrong for me to question the priest and the Catholic church. I wasn't supposed to want to know where my "faith" came from and what it was based on. Conflict and friction arose that led to more questions about how I saw my life in society compared to how others saw it. It was unacceptable to want to climb trees and play baseball like my brother. It was dumb to also feel like he should participate in the housework like my mom and I did; to expect him to do the dishes and tell him to bring me my food sometimes. I became a deviant in my own home for questioning these seemingly solid roles assigned to women and men. It was a "nuisance" when my predominantly African-American magnet high school was placed in a white neighborhood. It was expected of us to cause trouble in that neighborhood, and to be eventually pushed out of the town by the concerned residents. I realized my position in society through these and many other events in my life. I saw how, if I tried to oppose or break through the barriers that defined my role, I would immediately be seen as wrong, unacceptable, different, or deviant.

I experienced greater resistance when my pursuit was that of higher education. During my senior year of high school, I was encouraged to fill out a maximum of six college applications and a minimum of two. Throughout this process I consulted many of my teachers. One particular teacher, Mr. C., had become up to this point one of my best friends. He was also the performing arts teacher, and I was very much involved in performing arts. He taught me how to further my guitar skills, and always gave me books and music that he thought I would find interesting. When this period of transition came, I asked for his input on my decisions to apply to moderately and highly competitive schools. He looked me straight in the eye and told me that I was crazy to think that I would get into any competitive school. "I think you should apply to Southern [a state commuter school]. You are gonna be up against a lot of white rich kids coming from top schools with SAT scores of at least 1200," he said. In that moment I was reminded of who I was. I was "warned" to not try to go beyond what was expected of a Latina from the inner-city. What was "normal" for rich white kids became what was deviant for me. And in that one moment I decided to prove him and the rest of the "normal" world wrong. That Spring I was accepted into Boston College, my first choice, Vassar College, and Sarah Lawrence College. (I photocopied my Boston College acceptance letter and put it in Mr. C's mailbox).

41

When I arrived at Boston College, I underestimated to what extent my struggle would be with college life. Instead of driving straight through the gates towards my dorm, I had to go straight to More Hall, to clear up financial matters. While everyone else was carrying up boxes and futons, I was pleading for some type of financial arrangement. After signing many frustrating documents, I was finally allowed to move in. What I thought to be small and insignificant, were what defined who I was and who I could be at Boston College. The rituals of my daily life were confronted with resistance and were labeled deviant. I don't remember which situation or experience affected me first; whether it was the suspicious stares, or my roommate's massive amount of material items, or it it was simply the existence of too much difference. All of a sudden I felt very Hispanic. I felt very angry, alone and afraid. I began to wonder why my roommate came home every weekend with tons of bags from different department stores, yet always complained about not having enough. I wondered why no one else on my floor was constantly visiting the financial aid office and calling more sources for money for school. I began to feel the stigma of never having quite enough cash for pizza, movies, and cabs. I began to clearly see the divide when I had to stay in while others went out to spend money, to have fun. I had to get used to eating meals that I'd never had before and always wondered why I was the last, or almost last, person to be chosen to sit next to in class. My style of dress and talk were unfamiliar here. All the simple things in life for me, food, clothes, school, friends, money, became the most difficult. All these aspects demonstrated the magnitude of power and control and who possessed it. After the initial realization that I was extremely different from most of the students, I asserted my culture even more. I would blare merengue and salsa, and city (rap, hip-hop, and reggae) music while listening to soft rock or alternative music mainly through my walkman. I was not aware that my slang began to get thicker, and that I smiled mostly at minorities when walking by. I participated in almost every cultural event seeing it as my duty as a minority at Boston College. I dressed, acted and talked like a stereotypical Latina. My haughty disposition around the white students contrasted my welcoming, understanding nods at students of color. This first semester of my freshman year accounted for much depression and lack of self-knowledge. At no other point in my life have I had to significantly alter and re-alter my personality. It was during this time when concepts of deviance and social control seemed to appear sharper to me.

I survived that semester, the following one, and am trudging through the present one with no major scars or injuries. I still occassionally blare merengue and salsa, yet also am not ashamed of my taste for rock, pop, or alternative music. I am still not accustomed to the food here, though I am more open to trying it out. I live on a multi-cultural floor. I don't participate in every AHANA (umbrella organization for multi-cultural organizations at B.C.) event, and don't feel obliged to. Spiritually, I have left the Catholic church (tradition), and searched and found true (non-denominational) Christianity. I still make frequent visits to the financial aid office (next semester's tuition is looking grim), and scrounge for laundry money. And although I may still appear to be a deviant in this society, I am confident enough to say that "everyone else is just different." I do wonder about how different it would be if the tables were turned; if blaring merengue, eating arroz and pasteles, speaking Spanish, wearing baggy clothes, and paying for school with a summer job were the norm. It is obvious though that social control has a tendency to be irreversible. In order for any of my desires to feel as though I am truly a significant aspect of my society in the United States of America, I would have to change not only the existing circumstances of my position, but the entire course of history. My story of my freshman year experience was the result of institutions, ideas, and power enforced and taken hundreds of years ago. I didn't automatically become a deviant once I drove through the great gates of Boston College. I was always predetermined, expected to be that way. It is undeniable that my mother, and her mother, and the mother before all had a clear, distinct role and pattern to follow that would ensure their specifically designed position in society, and any alteration or divergence from that is wrong, abnormal, and deviant. Therefore, I conclude that in order for me to never be considered a deviant, I must conform to the pattern that the powerful have laid out for me, and until the power is shifted into others' hands there will always be a struggle among classes. I do not consider myself the victim, because I know that even through writing this paper I have labeled and stereotyped others. My pursuit to become educated has allowed me to recognize the barriers, and challenge them. I will continue to learn, question, challenge, and conform in order to survive. I have recognized my limits though am not afraid of surpassing them. I am not a social deviant nor a hostile product of my society; I am simply a person trying to live. I don't blame one thing or person for the inequality that exists, yet feel that there isn't an excuse for "putting up with it." I am not the bitter freshman walking down the dustbowl, but a female student still redefining my character through my experiences at Boston College and my experiences to come. Nowadays, whenever I walk by anyone who's making eye contact, I don't hesitate to smile.

"If theories about nonconformity were constructed by people whom society labels as deviants rather than by other who fear and attempt to control deviants, how different might the conceptual understandings be?"

Stephen Pfohl
IMAGES OF DEVIANCE AND
SOCIAL CONTROL

Heart

The rain shot down in grinding, cold pellets. Countless beads of sweat forced their way through every pore. The moisture drenched my blue uniform. I shifted my weight back from one bruised leg to another. The only thing I felt was the slippery, unstable ground under my feet. The pain came later. A whistle blew. The ball was out. My brow furrowed in intense concentration. I saw a goal; a white net of anticipation and purpose. The opponents were in front of me, frozen, in a mannequin state. I possessed a frame of mind, in those few seconds, similar to that of a warrior who saw nothing but the defeat of the enemy. The fight had been long and hard, and the only thing that mattered was the victory. Everything around me became blurry, meaningless. The goal in front of me was real. Determination was stronger than ever and there were no signs of backing down. My fists and jaw clenched. The whistle blew again. My joints immediately responded. Blood rushed to my head. I exploded with full force towards the goal. I barely heard the screeching fans on the sidelines when...

I played this soccer game during the fall of my junior year in high school. It was not a state, county or even city, championship game. *All right girls, let's see some heart out on that field today!* The fans consisted of a couple of soccer coaches, sprinkled with a few injured players, and maybe even a concerned parent of an asthmatic halfback. Our uniforms and equipment were basic, simple, and of low quality. *There's nothing we could do, girls. Budget's tight. Work with what you got.* It was a home game, yet were not playing on a home field because we did not have one. *Well, there's another zoning hearing tomorrow, maybe...* We had lost every game before this one. *Our Father, who art in heaven...* We had countless injuries and even more negative attitudes. *Why the hell should I play on this team. You can't make me do anything!* We also had to deal with the harsh realities of racism and prejudice. *Damn spics and niggers.* With 1 substitute player, and all the hardships we had suffered, we needed this win, badly. Many of the more committed team members had worked extremely hard all season. I was sick of watching our team walk off the field with their heads bowed in confusion, shame, and hopelessness. We had experienced our shares of sweat, blood, and tears. We had suffered immensely. We lived for the chance to prove ourselves worthy. And we had that one last game to do it. And we did.

That one rainy afternoon did not change my life forever. I did not make the winning goal. I don't have any soccer trophies lined up against the walls of our living room. I don't remember the names of everyone on the team. I do know that, in that one moment of victory, I saw an unfamiliar gleam of happiness in my goalie's eyes. I heard vigor and hope, not anger and frustration, in my coach's shouts. I felt adrenaline rushing through my bruised shins and ankles. It was in that one instant that I saw who I was and what I was truly capable of. I saw strength, determination, and passion. I saw how much I hated to lose. I saw challenges I faced when working with others. For the first time in my life, I had to learn how to work with people who sometimes did not see the need to really strive for excellence. I had to eventually lead them, as a captain, towards a goal they sometimes saw as impossible to reach. I also saw how much I needed the support of my team; how impossible it was to depend solely on myself. For the first time I saw myself fully responsible for every action on an off the field and the actions of my teammates. I saw my desperate need to create an unbreakable union amongst us in order to start winning some games. I saw how easily I ignored the pain, both the physical bruises and emotional scars of disappointment and frustration. And I realized how much I love the rain.

Instead of mud on a field, I am currently trudging through the second semester of my first year at Boston College. Sweat breaks out on my forehead and palms when I choose classes, meet new people, and take exams. The only numbers that are important now are the digits on my tuition bill. *Hey coach, I think you should retire my number.* The pain lies now in my stomach from too much take-out or McElroy food. The only whistle blowing now is that of my alarm clock signaling me to hurry to class. *Offside! Who hired that ref?* I still explode in full force, when I am late for class, or am making a dash for the Dunkin' Donuts line. *Load up on carbs, lots of rest,...* The fans, though fewer, are cheering loudly and consist of a few family members and a couple of close friends. *Good job, girls. Don't forget heart. Give it heart.* My current long-time goal is to obtain a masters degree in Social Work. *How are you holding up? Did you get that injury checked out?* It is not common for me to venture into the place in my mind where only memories exist, examine them, and think about how they affected me. I am in college now. There are new people, new experiences, new places, and new memories to make. There is also a new identity to create and establish. Throughout my investigations and discoveries, I have been able to begin to produce the beginning of a new me. The rigorous courses, diverse students and faculty, and new-found responsibilities have shaped me into a person who is ambitious, spirited, finds it difficult to work with others, recognizes the need for others, attempts to ignore pain, and adores the rain.

"...everything can be taken from a man but one thing: the last of the human freedoms—to chose one's attitude in any given set of circumstances, to choose one's own way."

Victor E. Frankl
MAN'S SEARCH FOR
MEANING

V.

Obituary

Gloribell Lopez died peacefully today of natural causes. She was 102. She leaves behind eight children, four grandchildren, three great-grandchildren, and a loving, faithful husband. She was a highly recognized person in her community, always volunteering and giving to the less fortunate in her area. She traveled all over the world helping feed the hungry, and also did a lot of sight-seeing with her husband and children. She was the author of one best-seller, and later gave up her writing career to get into the movie business. Never starring in any movies, she always managed to portray a certain amount of charm and mystery through her characters, which always left audiences begging for more. After receiving a multi-million dollar sample from Hollywood, she quickly retreated into a different field. Counseling and teaching at inner-city high schools became her niche. There she was a "mother-friend-homegirl" sort of person everyone loved. She enjoyed working with adolescents and retired at 55, at which time she bought a 34-foot Winnebago and spent the happiest years watching the rain and relaxing with her loving, faithful husband.

Constant Reminder

There was a constant reminder today.
One that has always been stressed,
and for good reason too (they say).
One that must keep me within the
fences that have been built up
around me.
Sure they don't want me to see
the fences, so they blindfold me
to make sure I won't see
my way out, see the other side.
Not that I would want
to get out. It's a good
place for me in here (they say).
With my kind.
I'm new here, but I know
how things work. You can't
think hard. They teach
us what is important to
know. That of course is
the constant reminder.
You can't wish or dream
either, although it is
hard for me to try and stop.
(They say) this is how we were
born, and this is how we'll die.
It's part of the constant reminder.
Everyone knows that.
Oh, and don't ask to fly.
I did, and the answer
wasn't what I had wanted.
Though we're not supposed to
want too much either.

The response from them
was first a loud, hearty laugh.
It kind of made me want to
smile. And I did, for a little
bit, but not too much because
then they pat you on the head
and walk away.
Kind of like pity.
Then came the constant reminder.
I knew it was coming.
I was just maybe hoping...
Hoping is foolishness for us (they say).
I'm a minority in more ways
than one. I am a woman. I am Hispanic.
I could never make it in this
world. I'm disadvantaged. All
the shots are against me. Low class.
And guess what, I
felt like crying, but
these words, this constant reminder
made me strong,
made me proud,
made me fly.

BIOGRAPHICAL NOTES

Gloribell Lopez was born in New Haven, Connecticut on November 8, 1978. Ms. Lopez grew up in the Fair Haven neighborhood of New Haven and attended Clinton Avenue, Columbus Elementary and Fair Haven Middle Schools. In 1993, she spent three weeks as an exchange student in Avignon, France. Ms. Lopez graduated with Honors as a member of the Hyde Leadership School's first graduating class in June of 1996, and is currently a Sociology major at Boston College.

Since an early age, Ms. Lopez's writing has reflected social concern. She wrote her first dramatic skits while in middle school. Her commentary piece **Many Factors Involved in Education** was published in <u>The Progeny: Voices of Greater New Haven Youth</u> in June of 1996.

At age 11, Ms. Lopez began guitar studies with Roberto Ortiz at Centro San José in New Haven and continues to play, incorporating Latin American standards and some original work in her repertoire. At age 12, she was a water color student of renowned Connecticut visual artist Tony Falcone and had her work "Chapel Square Mall" exhibited at the New Haven City Hall.

Starting at age 13, Ms. Lopez served as a volunteer at Centro San José. From 1991 to 1994, she served on the organizing committee of the Centro San José Discovery of Puerto Rico 2 Mile Road Race, and was Race Starter of the event in 1994.

While at Hyde, Ms. Lopez played soccer, ran track and was on the self-defense team. In 1995, she was featured as a Rising Star in the Inner City newspaper and was crowned Miss Puerto Rico-New Haven.